MEOW!

KIDS ASK ABOUT

KITTENS

HOW are kittens born?

WHEN do kittens start walking?

WHO are kittens' relatives?

Written by Christopher Nicholas
Illustrated by Alaskan Moose Studios

sequoia® children's publishing
An imprint of PHOENIX International Publications, Inc.
Chicago • London • Hamburg • Mexico City • Sydney

Visit us at
SequoiaKidsBooks.com
for bonus
downloadable content

Photo credits © 2025 Shutterstock.com: beton studio; Megan Betteridge; Butterfly Hunter; Tony Campbell; Linn Curries; DenisNata; evgeniaborodinova; GoodFocused; Eric Isselee; Dmitry Kalinovsky; Khorzhevska; Rita_Kochmarjova; Krakenimages.com; Puttachat Kumkrong; Andrey_Kuzmin; Oleksandr Lytvynenko; Nadezhda Molkentin; oksana2010; Tom Pingel; ANURAK PONGPATIMET; Reidl; Ryan Chin; Sviatoslav_Shevchenko; Jesus Souto; StockPhotosArt; Arsenenko Svitlana; Galyna Syngaievska; Tsekhmister; Nynke van Holten

Published by Sequoia Children's Publishing,
an imprint of Sequoia Publishing & Media, LLC

Sequoia Publishing & Media, LLC,
a division of Phoenix International Publications, Inc.

8501 West Higgins Road, Chicago, Illinois 60631
34 Seymour Street, London W1H 7JE
Heimhuder Straße 81, 20148 Hamburg

CustomerService@PhoenixInternational.com

www.PhoenixInternational.com

Library of Congress Control Number: 2022920283

ISBN: 978-1-64269-459-8

KIDS ASK ABOUT

KITTENS

TABLE OF CONTENTS

WHO are kittens?

Kittens are very young cats, just like children are very young people. Kittens are mammals like humans. This means that when they are babies, they feed on their mothers' milk.

WHO are kittens' relatives?

As members of the cat family, kittens are related to lions, tigers, leopards, cheetahs, and other big cats that live in the wild. But most kittens are domesticated. That means, unlike their wild cousins, they live with and depend on people to take care of them.

WHAT do kittens look like?

All kittens are covered with hair, called fur, which protects them by keeping them warm and dry. Their ears allow them to hear high-pitched sounds that humans can't hear, like a mouse squeaking. They have four legs and four fuzzy feet, called paws. But watch out! Kittens also have sharp claws to help them climb, hunt, and fight.

HOW do kittens use their tails?

Kittens' tails help them keep their balance when climbing and jumping—like how holding out your arms can help you walk across a balance beam.

KITTEN BODY PARTS:

- Four legs and paws
- Claws
- Whiskers
- Four canines (long, pointy teeth)

DID YOU KNOW?

Kittens are specially equipped for the dark. Big, shiny eyes help them see better, and long whiskers act as “feelers” to help them find their way.

HOW many types of kittens are there?

There are more than 70 different kinds, or breeds, of kittens in the world. Each breed has a very distinctive size, shape, fur length, and color. But all the breeds fall under two types: long-haired and short-haired.

LONG-HAIRED KITTENS

DID YOU KNOW?
Some kittens barely have hair at all!
Sphynx
Blue British shorthair
Siamese
SHORT-HAIRED KITTENS

HOW are kittens born?

When a mother cat is ready to have her kittens, she finds a safe, quiet place, such as under a bed or inside a closet. The mother cat can give birth to as many as seven or eight kittens—two to six is more typical. Together, the kittens are called a litter.

KITTEN FACTS:

- Born one at a time
- Average litter: 2-6

HOW do kittens get clean?

Mother cats lick their kittens to bathe them and teach them how to clean their own fur when they get older. To bathe themselves, cats and older kittens lick their paws and use them to wash areas like their heads and faces where their tongues can't reach.

DID YOU KNOW?

Licking also helps kittens' skin glands produce more body oil to waterproof their coat. That's why they're always so shiny!

WHAT do kittens eat?

When they are first born, kittens mostly drink milk from their mothers. By the time they're eight weeks old, they are big enough to eat solid food—either kitten food from their pet owners or small animals caught by their mothers.

KITTEN FOOD:

- Mother's milk
- Packaged kitten food
- Small animals

HOW do kittens grow?

Little by little—just like you do! Newborn kittens weigh 3 to 4 ounces (85–113.4 grams), and they are so tiny that you can hold one in the palm of your hand. They are born with their eyes and ears closed but have a good sense of smell.

WHEN do kittens' eyes and ears open?

In a week, newborn kittens grow twice their original size! Then, nine to 20 days later, their eyes and ears begin to open. Because newborn kittens cannot stand or walk, the mother cat carries them around in her mouth.

WHEN do kittens start walking?

After four weeks, kittens stand and slowly begin to walk. Still wobbly, they wander off and explore. But mom always keeps a close cat eye on them! By eight to 12 weeks, kittens' bodies are longer and stronger. They can run, play, and get into all kinds of kitty mischief.

KITTEN DEVELOPMENT:

4 weeks
- Stand
- Walk

8-12 weeks
- Run
- Play

6 months
- Nearly full-grown
- Independent

WHEN do kittens become cats?

After six months, kittens are nearly full-grown. They can do everything that adult cats can do! And they are ready to take care of themselves and lead their own cat lives.

WHY do kittens play so much?

Because it comes naturally to them. Cats and kittens that live in the wild hunt mice and other small animals for food. So domestic kittens that chase balls, poke in and out of boxes, and climb on curtains are actually practicing mouse hunting!

KITTEN BEHAVIOR:

- Naturally curious
- Playful (practice for hunting and fighting)

DID YOU KNOW?

When kittens wrestle with each other, they are learning how to protect themselves from other animals.

HOW do kittens communicate?

In many different ways. You just have to listen—and look! Kittens meow to say "hello," or to ask for something. And they purr when they are happy. When they're scared or angry, kittens hiss, puff out their fur, and arch their backs to make themselves look bigger—and scarier. Kittens' ears and tails can also show you what they're thinking.

EARS

Up and forward = happy

Back = angry

Flat = afraid

DID YOU KNOW?

Kittens also use smells to communicate. They rub against people and things to leave their scent and mark their territory. It says to other animals, "This is mine. Stay away!"

TAIL

Straight and high = happy

Down = sad or scared

Waving = excited or nervous

KITTEN TALK:

- Sounds
- Body movements
- Scents

DID YOU KNOW?

Kittens can see in light six times dimmer than people.

Kittens can pull in, or retract, their front claws.

Kittens almost always land on their feet! They have a special organ in their middle ear that helps them tell which side is up.

Kittens are great at climbing up, but they have a very hard time climbing down.

Kittens' whiskers grow to be a little longer than the width of their bodies.

KITTENS ARE AMAZING!

They have been our companions since they were first domesticated thousands of years ago. They were even seen as vessels for gods in ancient Egypt! Kittens are tons of furry fun, but always remember to play nice—you wouldn't want to make their big cousins angry!

MEOW!

MEOW!